Go to **www.ketoveo.com** for more guides and resources to help you on your keto journey.

Table of contents

MEXICAN ESSENTIALS

TORTILLAS
(Aztec: tlaxcalli = little cake)

Servings: 8

Nutritional Facts Per Serving:

Carbs:	4 g	Protein:	3 g
Fats:	6 g	Calories:	89 kcal

INGREDIENTS

3½ oz almond flour

1 tbsp coconut flour

2 tsp xanthan gum

1 tsp baking powder

¼ tsp salt

2 tsp apple cider vinegar

1 egg lightly beaten

3 tsp water

Notes:

One very important thing: when cooking, coconut flour burns rather rapidly. So while this does help you to get the traditional charred marks of flour tortillas, you do need to keep an eye out for them to keep them from burning. Having said that, you do want your skillet to be very hot in order for the tortillas to cook quickly (less than a minute) and stay pliable. Like any tortilla, if the heat is not high enough it will harden and crack.

This is how you make the recipe

1. Add almond flour, coconut flour, xanthan gum, baking powder and salt to food processor. Pulse until thoroughly combined.

2. Pour in apple cider vinegar with the food processor running. Once it has distributed evenly, pour in the egg, followed by the water. Stop the food processor once the dough forms into a ball. The dough will be sticky to touch.

3. Wrap dough in cling film and knead it through the plastic for a minute or two. Allow dough to rest for 10 minutes.

4. Heat up a skillet over medium heat. You can determine the proper heat by sprinkling on a few water droplets. If the drops evaporate immediately your pan is too hot. The droplets should skitter around the skillet.

5. Break the dough into eight 1-inch balls. Roll out between two sheets of parchment paper with a rolling pin or using a tortilla press (easier!) until each round is 5-inches in diameter.

6. Transfer to skillet and cook over medium heat for just 3-6 seconds (very important). Flip it over immediately, using a thin spatula or knife, and continue to cook until just lightly golden on each side about 30 to 40 seconds. The key is not to overcook them, as they will no longer be pliable or puff up.

7. Keep them warmly wrapped in a kitchen towel until ready to serve. To rewarm, heat briefly on both sides, until just warm (less than a minute).

8. These tortillas are best eaten while fresh. But feel free to keep some dough handy in your fridge for up to three days.

FRIJOLES REFRITOS
(Spanish: Refried beans)

Servings: 8

Nutritional Facts Per Serving:

Carbs:	3.2 g	Protein:	5.8 g
Fats:	5.6 g	Calories:	93 kcal

INGREDIENTS

1 eggplant (about 4 cups cubed)
4 slices bacon
1 cup chopped yellow onions
1 tbsp minced garlic
1 tbsp minced and seeded jalapeño
1 tbsp chile powder
1 tsp ground cumin
½ tsp Celtic sea salt
½ tsp chopped oregano
½ cup grated queso blanco (white cheese) or ricotta (optional)
¼ cup minced fresh cilantro, garnish (optional)
Pinch cayenne

This is how you make the recipe

1. Peel and cube the eggplant. Place cubes and 4 slices of uncooked bacon pieces in a pan. Stir fry until bacon is fried and eggplant is very very soft (about 10 minutes). Reserve bacon fat.

2. Place the eggplant (and bacon) in a food processor and puree until smooth.

3. In a large, heavy skillet, heat the bacon fat over medium-high heat. Add the onions and cook, stirring, until soft, about 3 minutes.

4. Add the garlic, jalapeño, chile powder, cumin, salt, and cayenne, and cook, stirring, until fragrant, about 45-60 seconds.

5. Add the eggplant puree and any cooking liquid from the pot, and the oregano, and stir to combine. Cook, stirring with a wooden spoon, until the mixture forms a thick paste, 5 to 10 minutes, adding water 1 tbsp at a time to keep from getting dry. Sprinkle with the cheese and cilantro, and serve.

ARROZ MEXICANO
(Spanish: Mexican rice)

Servings: 3			
Nutritional Facts Per Serving:			
Carbs:	3.5 g	Protein:	3 g
Fats:	5 g	Calories:	87 kcal

INGREDIENTS

Cauliflower rice:
½ head cauliflower
3 oz butter
½ tsp salt

Arroz Mexicano:
3 oz butter
1½ tsp garlic powder
3 tsp onion flakes
½ tsp pepper
½ tsp salt
2 cups cauliflower rice
¼ cup tomato puree
2 tsp cilantro, finely chopped

This is how you make the recipe

1. Cauliflower rice: Cut the cauliflower into evenly sized florets and place into your food processor, only filling half the bowl at a time.

2. Blend the cauliflower using the pulse setting. Continue to pulse until it resembles rice. If there are any large pieces, remove them and blend them separately.

3. Heat a frying pan over medium-low heat.

4. Add the butter and salt, allow the butter to melt before adding the cauliflower.

5. Saute the cauliflower for 5-8 minutes, while continually stirring.

6. Remove from heat.

1. Arroz Mexicano: Place a large frying pan over medium- low heat. Add the butter, garlic powder and onion flakes and gently sauté for 3 minutes.

2. Add the cauliflower rice, salt and pepper and sauté for 3 minutes, until the cauliflower is beginning to soften.

3. Add the tomato puree and stir well. Continue to cook for another 3-5 minutes until the cauliflower is cooked through.

4. Take the pan off the heat and stir through the cilantro.

5. Serve and enjoy.

SALSA ROJA
(Spanish: red sauce)

Servings: 2 cups

Nutritional Facts Per Serving:

Carbs:	7 g	Protein:	1 g
Fats:	0 g	Calories:	33 kcal

INGREDIENTS

8 medium tomatoes

2-3 chili peppers

4 cloves garlic

1 tbsp salt

2 limes, juiced

This is how you make the recipe

1. Roast tomatoes, chili pepper and garlic by grilling on high 5-8 minutes on each side until the skin on the veggies begins to burn and peel away.

2. Allow veggies to cool for 5 minutes.

3. Add these roasted veggies to a blender. Add salt and lime juice. Pulse 4-6 times until salsa reaches desired consistency

4. Store in an airtight container up to 7 days in the refrigerator.

SALSA VERDE
(Spanish: Green sauce)

Servings: 3 cups			
Nutritional Facts Per Serving:			
Carbs:	5 g	Protein:	6 g
Fats:	3 g	Calories:	52 kcal

INGREDIENTS

12 oz green tomatillos

1 clove garlic

1-3 jalapeño or serrano peppers, halved and seeded

½ oz fresh cilantro

⅔ cup onion, cut into three parts

1 avocado

This is how you make the recipe

1. Add green tomatillos, garlic clove, ⅓ of the onion and chile to a medium saucepan over medium/low heat. Combine with enough water just to cover, and bring to a boil. Lower the heat to low and simmer for 6 to 7 minutes.

2. Drain cooked salsa ingredients and place in a food processor, with remaining raw onion, fresh cilantro, avocado and ½ tsp salt to start until smooth.

TACO SEASONING

Servings: 6-12			
Nutritional Facts Per Serving:			
Carbs:	1 g	Protein:	0.2 g
Fats:	0 g	Calories:	5 kcal

INGREDIENTS

1 tbsp ground chile powder

1½ tsp ground cumin

1 tsp paprika

½ tsp granulated garlic

½ tsp granulated onion

½ tsp dried oregano, rubbed

½ tsp salt

¼ tsp pepper

1 tsp Swerve Granulated

This is how you make the recipe

1. Measure all of the ingredients into a small bowl and whisk with a fork. Keep in a airtight container.

2. This recipe makes 1/4 cup of seasoning. You may use the whole recipe for 1 pound of ground beef or half of the recipe (2 tbsp per pound of meat) depending on your taste.

TACO SAUCE

Servings: 6

Nutritional Facts Per Serving:

Carbs:	2.2 g	Protein:	1.9 g
Fats:	0.1 g	Calories:	18 kcal

INGREDIENTS

8 oz can tomato sauce

¼ cup water

3 tbsp taco seasoning (see recipe above)

1 tbsp white vinegar

1 tbsp dried onion flakes

This is how you make the recipe

1. In a medium saucepan, over medium heat, combine all ingredients.

2. Bring to a boil over medium, reduce to low, and simmer. Simmer for 5-10 minutes, stirring occasionally.

RED ENCHILADA SAUCE

Servings: 8

Nutritional Facts Per Serving:
Carbs: 2 g   Protein: 2 g
Fats: 2 g   Calories: 53 kcal

INGREDIENTS

3 cups unsalted chicken broth
3 tbsp tomato paste
1 whole bay leaf
2 tbsp pure chile powder
1 tbsp sweet paprika
2 tsp ground cumin
1 tsp dried oregano
½ tsp salt
½ tsp granulated garlic
½ tsp onion powder
½ tsp Swerve
¼ tsp chipotle chile powder
¼ tsp instant coffee powder
Pinch ground clove
Pinch ground cinnamon

This is how you make the recipe

1. Put all of the ingredients into a medium to large frying pan on medium heat.

2. Simmer gently, stirring occasionally, until the red enchilada sauce has reduced by 1 cup and about 2 cups are left. (The burner heat may need to be adjusted) The sauce will be thin but flavorful. It will thicken-up in the oven as the enchiladas cook.

3. Remember: The enchilada sauce is what flavors the enchiladas, so taste and adjust the seasonings. If the sauce is a little bitter, add just a touch more sweetener. It will help balance the flavors, but go easy with it. Discard the bay leaf before using.

GUACAMOLE
*(Aztec: āhuacatl = avocado &
mōlli = sauce)*

Servings: 4			
Nutritional Facts Per Serving:			
Carbs:	6.6 g	Protein:	3.7 g
Fats:	22.2 g	Calories:	262 kcal

INGREDIENTS

3 avocados

3 tbsp olive oil

2 cloves garlic, minced

2 tbsp lime juice

Dash of Tabasco sauce

¼ red or white onion, finely diced

2 Roma tomatoes, seeded, and finely diced

1-2 tbsp cilantro, finely chopped

salt and pepper

This is how you make the recipe

1. Put avocados, olive oil, garlic, lime juice, Tabasco, salt and pepper in a large bowl. Mash together thoroughly with a potato masher or fork.

2. Fold in the rest of the ingredients and add salt and pepper to taste.

MOLE POBLANO
(Aztec: mōlli = sauce,
Spanish: Poblano = from Puebla)

Servings: 6 cups			
Nutritional Facts Per Serving:			
Carbs:	2.6 g	Protein:	0.63 g
Fats:	3.4 g	Calories:	47 kcal

INGREDIENTS

1 tbsp pecan nuts

1 tbsp sesame seeds

1 tbsp pumpkin seeds

1 tbsp peanuts

1 tbsp almonds

2 guajillo chile

2 pasilla chile

2 ancho chile

½ tomato

¼ onion

1 clove garlic

½ tsp black pepper

1 whole bay leaf

1 clove

½ tsp cumin

2 cups chicken soup

1 oz 80% dark chocolate

2 tsp Swerve

salt to taste

Coconut oil

This is how you make the recipe

1. In a frying pan, with a little bit of coconut oil, put 1 tbsp of pecan nuts, 1 tbsp sesame seeds, 1 tbsp pumpkin seeds,1 tbsp peanuts, 1tbsp almonds and roast all of them.

2. Roast 2 guajillo chile, 2 pasilla chile, and 2 ancho chiles and then put the chiles in hot water. When the chiles are soft, remove the seeds.

3. Roast ½ tomato, ¼ onion, and 1 clove of garlic with ½ tsp of black pepper, 1 bay leaf, 1 clove and ½ tsp cumin. Do not add salt yet; it comes at the end. Remove the bay leaf.

4. Put all the ingredients in a blender with 2 cups of chicken soup. Mix it for at least 5 minutes.

5. Heat a bit of oil in a casserole and stir in all of the sauce. The secret to this recipe is that you have to stir it all the time, with a wood or plastic spoon, over very low heat, for at least 30 minutes.

6. Then add the dark chocolate and Swerve.

7. Keep moving the sauce for another 30 minutes until become thicken. Add more chicken soup if you need it. Add salt as needed.

MEXICAN COLESLAW WITH LIME DRESSING

Servings: 6

Nutritional Facts Per Serving:

Carbs:	6 g	Protein:	2 g
Fats:	10 g	Calories:	137 kcal

INGREDIENTS

Mexican Coleslaw:
1 lb white cabbage
1 lb red cabbage
2 carrots
1/3 cup chopped cilantro

Lime Dressing:
2 tbsp lime juice
1 tsp ground cumin
¼ cup olive oil
salt/pepper to taste
1 spring onion, sliced

This is how you make the recipe

1. Mexican Coleslaw: Using a food processor and the shredding/grating blade, shred the cabbage and carrots.

2. Place in a large serving dish.

1. Lime Dressing: Place all the ingredients for the lime dressing in a bowl. Whisk with a fork.

2. Pour over the Mexican coleslaw.

3. Gently stir to combine.

BREAKFAST

HUEVOS RANCHEROS

Servings: 2

Nutritional Facts Per Serving:

Carbs:	0.5 g	Protein:	7.3 g
Fats:	5 g	Calories:	78 kcal

INGREDIENTS

Tortillas:
Coconut oil, for frying
3 egg, separated
2 tbsp egg white protein or whey protein
2 tbsp cream cheese, very soft
1 tsp onion powder

Toppings:
½ cup browned grass fed beef
Fried eggs
Avocado
Salsa
Green onions
Peppers

This is how you make the recipe

1. Place the egg whites (no yolk at all or it won't work) in a bowl and whip with a hand mixer or stand mixer until they are very stiff.

2. Slowly add in the unflavored protein powder and spices.

3. Then gently stir in the cream cheese or yolks.

4. Heat oil in a small skillet over medium-high heat.

5. Fry tortilla dough one at a time until firm, but not crisp.

6. Remove onto paper towels to drain excess oil.

7. Meanwhile, prepare the beef and other desired topping.

8. When tortillas are done, fry eggs over-easy in the skillet.

9. Place tortillas onto plates, and spread a layer of meat on them.

10. Top with your desired toppings.

CHILAQUILES
(Aztec: chilaquilitl = to put in chilies)

Servings: 4			
Nutritional Facts Per Serving:			
Carbs:	7 g	Protein:	10 g
Fats:	15 g	Calories:	222 kcal

INGREDIENTS

6 tortillas (see the Mexican Essentials section)
1 cup salsa verde (see the Mexican Essentials section)
2 tbsp avocado oil
1-4 fried or scrambled eggs
¼ cup red onion, thinly sliced
small handful fresh cilantro, roughly chopped
Queso fresco
Fresh limes
Red pepper flakes
Salsa verde

This is how you make the recipe

1. Preheat the oven to 400°F.

2. Lightly grease a baking sheet with 1 tbsp of avocado oil.

3. Cut the tortillas into 6 equal wedges and arrange in a single layer on the baking sheet. Brush the tops with the remaining avocado oil. Sprinkle with sea salt and black pepper.

4. Bake for 10-15 minutes until golden brown and crispy, turning the pan halfway through. Remove from the oven and allow to cool.

5. To prepare the chilaquiles, place the chips on a serving platter. Spoon the salsa verde evenly over top. Use as much or as little as you'd like. Top with red onion, cilantro, egg(s) and finally, sprinkle the cheese (is using) evenly over top. Enjoy immediately.

BIRRIA

Servings: 4			
Nutritional Facts Per Serving:			
Carbs:	3 g	Protein:	21.6 g
Fats:	6.7 g	Calories:	164 kcal

INGREDIENTS

4 guajillo chiles
4 Poblano chiles
1 cup hot water
1 lb top round, cubed for stew
1 lb baby-back ribs, cut into 1-inch
pieces
2½ qts water
1 onion
6 garlic cloves
2 whole fresh bay leaves
6 sprigs thyme
1 tbsp ground cumin
1 tbsp Mexican oregano (not Italian
oregano)
Salt and pepper

Sauce:
½ cup red wine vinegar
2 garlic cloves
1 tsp ground piquin chile

Garnish:
½ cup diced onion
2 limes, cut into wedges
½ cup chopped cilantro

This is how you make the recipe

1. On hot griddle toast the Poblano and guajillo chile and submerge in hot water. Let chiles sit for 20 minutes. Remove from water and puree in blender with a cup of warm water. Set aside.

2. In a deep dutch oven or 6-quart stock pot, add the beef and ribs, water, onion, and garlic cloves. Bring to boil and cook for 1 hour. At this point add the bay leaves, thyme, chiles puree, cumin, oregano, salt, and pepper simmer for 30 minutes. Remove the bay leaf.

3. To make sauce, puree the garlic, vinegar, and chile powder in a blender.

4. Serve the stew in a big bowl with a sprinkle of onion and cilantro and a squeeze of lime on top. Serve with corn tortillas and some of the sauce on the side, as well.

DESAYUNO CAZUELA
(Spanish: Breakfast casserole)

Servings: 6			
Nutritional Facts Per Serving:			
Carbs:	5.6 g	Protein:	26.4 g
Fats:	31.8 g	Calories:	423 kcal

INGREDIENTS

1 lb thick-cut bacon

2 tbsp reserved bacon grease or ghee

1 small turnip, diced

1 large red onion, thinly sliced

3 cups spinach

12 large eggs

⅓ cup whole milk

1 tsp salt

1 tsp garlic powder

½ tsp black pepper

½ cup shredded cheddar cheese

Notes:

A small amount of whole milk can be used. However, if you want to avoid milk, you can use a combination of 1 tbsp heavy whipping cream mixed with 1/4 cup water.

This is how you make the recipe

1. Preheat the oven to 400˚F. Cut the bacon into 2 inch pieces and arrange on a parchment lined baking sheet. Bake for 15 minutes until crisp, ant then remove from the oven. You can use the bacon grease for greasing the pan in the next step.

2. Heat the reserved bacon grease in a medium pan over medium-high heat. Add in the turnip and onion, cook until soft about 5-7 minutes.

3. Transfer to a 9 x 13 inch baking dish. Top the turnip and onion with the spinach.

4. Whisk together the eggs, milk, and spices. Pour over the spinach.

5. Sprinkle the cheese across the top then arrange the bacon in a single layer across the top of the casserole.

6. Transfer to the oven and bake 20-25 minutes or until the eggs are set. Serve.

CHILE RELLENOS

Servings: 8

Nutritional Facts Per Serving:

Carbs:	6 g	Protein:	16 g
Fats:	29 g	Calories:	365 kcal

INGREDIENTS

8 large Poblano peppers
12 large portabella mushrooms
1 lb pepper jack cheese
½ cup sour cream
½ cup heavy cream
½ tsp mineral salt

This is how you make the recipe

1. Slit the peppers lengthwise and horizontally at the top. Remove the seeds. Roast in a large dish at 450˚F for 20-25 minutes. The peppers will start to darken, wilt, and blister.

2. Chop the mushrooms into quarters. Sauté in a pan on medium/high heat for 10 minutes. The mushrooms will shrink and release their moisture.

3. Mix the mushrooms, cheese, sour cream, heavy cream, salt, and optional spices in a bowl. Stuff this mixture into the baked peppers and pile any extra on top. Bake the stuffed peppers for another 15 minutes. The cheese will melt and turn golden brown.

4. Garnish the chile rellenos with chopped green onions, cilantro, sour cream, chorizo, and more.

CROCK-POT PORK CHILE VERDE

Servings: 8			
Nutritional Facts Per Serving:			
Carbs:	7 g	Protein:	44 g
Fats:	17 g	Calories:	376 kcal

INGREDIENTS

For the sauce:
1 lb tomatillos, husked and halved
2 Poblano peppers, halved and seeded
2 jalapeño peppers, halved and seeded
2 tbsp avocado oil
1 onion, quartered
4 cloves garlic
Small handful fresh cilantro
Juice of 2 limes
2 tsp cumin
1 tsp chile powder
1 tsp red pepper flakes
1 tsp salt
1 tsp oregano
Salt and pepper to taste

For the rest:
4 lb pork butt or shoulder
8 cups greens (romaine, spinach, etc.)
4 cups arroz Mexicano (see the Mexican Essentials section) (optional)

Notes:

You can prepare the sauce in advance, just complete steps 2-5 below and store the sauce in an airtight container in the fridge until you are ready to throw everything in the slow cooker.

This is how you make the recipe

1. Preheat your oven to 400°F. Another note: If you want to get an extra smoky flavor, you can roast your tomatillos and peppers on a grill instead of the oven.

2. Prepare the tomatillos, Poblano and jalapeño peppers as noted and place them in a bowl. Toss with oil and a couple of generous pinches of salt and pepper.

3. Place the tomatillos and peppers cut side down on a baking sheet (or grill) and roast for 30 minutes. You want everything to develop a nice char on the outside, that's what gives the sauce the smoky flavor.

4. Next, place the roasted veggies in a blender. Add in the remaining sauce ingredients except salt and pepper and blend into a smooth consistency. Taste and add any salt and pepper to your liking.

5. Place the pork butt or shoulder in your crock-pot. Pour the chile verde sauce on top of the pork. Cook on low for 8-10 hours.

6. Prepare the arroz Mexicano, if you are having it.

7. Remove the pork from the crock-pot and shred it with 2 forks.

8. Spoon a generous amount of the sauce over the pork for serving. Serve pork over a bed of greens and arroz Mexicano (optional). Or, you can use for tacos! Enjoy!

GROUND BEEF BURRITO
(Spanish: Burro+ito = little donkey)

Servings: 12

Nutritional Facts Per Serving:
Carbs: 6.5 g Protein: 33 g
Fats: 20 g Calories: 365 kcal

INGREDIENTS

Beef Filling:
1 tbsp coconut oil
1 small yellow onion (diced)
2 cloves minced garlic
1 lb ground beef (80% lean)
1 (14-oz) can diced tomatoes
1 tbsp ground cumin
1 tbsp dried coriander
1 tsp chile powder
1 tsp paprika
1 tsp dried oregano

Wraps:
3 large eggs
12 large egg whites (very fresh)
3 tbsp coconut flour
1½ tbsp ground psyllium husk
5 tbsp unsweetened almond milk
¾ tsp baking soda
1½ tsp cream tartar
Coconut oil

Toppings:
Salsa Roja or salsa verde (see the Mexican Essentials section)
shredded cheese (to serve)
Diced Avocado (to serve)
sour cream (to serve)

This is how you make the recipe

1. Heat the oil in a large skillet over medium-high heat.

2. Add the onions and garlic and cook for 3 minutes, stirring often.

3. Stir in the ground beef and cook until it is browned, breaking it up with a spoon.

4. Add the diced tomatoes and spices then stir well.

5. Simmer for 15 minutes on low heat while you prepare the wraps.

6. Combine the eggs, egg whites, coconut flour, psyllium husk, almond milk, baking soda, and cream of tartar in a mixing bowl.

7. Whisk until well combined then let rest for 10 minutes and whisk again.

8. Heat a large nonstick skillet over medium heat and grease with coconut oil.

9. Pour in just enough batter to coat the bottom of the skillet, tilting it to spread evenly.

10. Cook until the bottom of the wrap is set then carefully flip it and cook until just browned on the other side.

11. Remove the wrap to a plate and cover to keep warm.

12. Repeat with the remaining wrap batter – you should have about 12 wraps.

13. Spoon the cooked beef into the wraps and top with shredded cheese, avocado, salsa and sour cream.

14. Roll the wraps up around the fillings to serve.

CHILE RELLENO DE GUAJOLOTE

(Spanish: peppers stuffed with ground turkey)

Servings: 4			
Nutritional Facts Per Serving:			
Carbs:	8 g	Protein:	34 g
Fats:	28 g	Calories:	429 kcal

INGREDIENTS

1 tbsp olive oil

4 Poblano peppers

1 lb ground turkey

2 cloves garlic, minced

1 tbsp chili powder

1 tsp cumin

1 tsp paprika

1 red pepper, diced

1 red onion, diced

½ cup shredded cheddar cheese

Salsa Roja or salsa verde (see the Mexican Essentials section) (optional)

Sliced avocado (optional)

Cilantro (optional)

Sour cream (optional)

This is how you make the recipe

1. Preheat oven to 400°F. Wash and de-seed Poblano peppers, then drizzle with olive oil and season with salt and pepper if desired. Add to a parchment-lined baking sheet and bake for 10 minutes.

2. Meanwhile, cook ground beef over medium-high heat until browned, about 5-7 minutes.

3. Add chili powder, cumin, paprika, salt, garlic, red pepper and red onion, sautéing another 2 minutes until veggies are tender.

4. Stuff ground beef mixture into Poblano peppers, then top with cheese. Bake another 10 minutes until cheese is melted.

5. Remove from oven and top with toppings of choice. Serve and enjoy!

FAJITAS EL BISTEC
(Spanish: Little strips of beef steak)

Servings: 6		
Nutritional Facts Per Serving:		
Carbs:	4 g	Protein: 31 g
Fats:	33 g	Calories: 440 kcal

INGREDIENTS

2 cloves garlic, crushed

1 onion, sliced thin

½ tsp chili powder or more to taste

1 tbsp ground cumin powder

4 tbsp coconut oil or olive oil

1 lime juice and zest

1 lemon juice and zest

2 lb steak, sliced into strips

1 red pepper, sliced

1 yellow pepper, sliced

salt & pepper to taste

This is how you make the recipe

1. Mix all the ingredients together in the sheet pan/ baking tray.

2. Bake at 350°F for 15 minutes. Stir half way through cooking so the fajitas are cooked and mixed thoroughly.

3. Serve on Mexican coleslaw with lime dressing, or on a simple green salad with lime juice and oil drizzled over.

TAQUITOS

Servings: 6			
Nutritional Facts Per Serving:			
Carbs:	2.6 g	Protein:	19.6 g
Fats:	11 g	Calories:	188 kcal

INGREDIENTS

1 tbsp coconut oil

¼ onion, finely chopped

2 garlic cloves, minced

½ tsp cumin

½ tsp chile powder

1½ cup shredded chicken

⅓ cup enchilada sauce (see recipe in Mexican Essentials section)

2 tbsp freshly chopped cilantro, plus more for garnish

Kosher salt

1 cup shredded cheddar

1 cup shredded Monterrey jack

Sour cream

This is how you make the recipe

1. Preheat oven to 375˚F and line a small baking sheet with parchment paper.

2. Heat up the oil in a medium skillet over medium heat. Add onion and cook until slightly soft, about 3 minutes.

3. Add garlic and spices and cook until fragrant, 1 to 2 minutes more.

4. Add chicken and enchilada sauce, then bring mixture to a simmer. Stir in cilantro, season with salt, and remove from heat.

5. Make taquito shells: In a medium bowl, mix the cheeses together. Divide mixture into 6 piles on prepared baking sheet. Bake 8 to 10 minutes, or until cheese is melted and slightly golden around the edges. Let cool 2 to 4 minutes

6. Add a small pile of chicken and roll tightly. Repeat until all taquitos are made.

7. Garnish with cilantro and serve with sour cream, for dipping.

ARROZ CON POLLO
(Spanish: Rice with chicken)

Servings: 4			
Nutritional Facts Per Serving:			
Carbs:	8 g	Protein:	28 g
Fats:	16 g	Calories:	303 kcal

INGREDIENTS

2 large chicken breasts
1 tbsp coconut oil
2 tbsp taco seasoning (see the Mexican Essentials section)
4 cups arroz Mexicano (see the Mexican Essentials section)

To serve:
¼ cup shredded cheese
2 avocados

This is how you make the recipe

1. Heat coconut oil in a non-stick pan over medium heat.

2. Add the arroz Mexicano. Cook for about five minutes until it's slightly softened (you want it to maintain some crunch).

3. Remove from heat.

4. Add another 1 tbsp of coconut oil to the pan. Add bell peppers and onion, and cook for about five minutes, until slightly softened.

5. Remove from heat.

6. To prepare the chicken, slice horizontally to make two thin pieces from each chicken breast. Brush with oil and sprinkle with taco seasoning.

7. Add chicken to the pan and cook 4-5 minutes per side. Remove from heat, cover and allow to rest in the pan for five minutes.

8. Heat until steaming hot and cheese is melted over the chicken.

9. Add sliced avocado if desired.

TACO DIP

Servings: 12			
Nutritional Facts Per Serving:			
Carbs:	4 g	Protein:	7 g
Fats:	16 g	Calories:	389 kcal

INGREDIENTS

8 oz ground sirloin

2 avocados

10 oz can Ro-tel fire roasted tomatoes, drained

1 cup cheddar jack cheese, shredded

12 oz sour cream

1 oz sliced black olives

1 fresh jalapeño

Sliced cheddar and pepper jack cheese, for chips

1 tbsp cumin

1 tsp chile powder

1 tsp garlic powder

1 tsp onion powder

This is how you make the recipe

1. Pre-heat the oven to 350°F.

2. On a large baking sheet place parchment paper on top to prevent cheese from sticking to the baking sheet.

3. Take sliced cheeses and cut them into triangle shaped quarters. depending on how large your baking sheet is will determine how many of these you can cook at a time.

4. Bake the cheese triangles in the oven for about 8 to 9 minutes and remove and place on counter for a couple minutes to begin cooling.

5. Before the cheese triangles are completely cooled off blot them with a paper towel to remove excess grease from the top and then put them on top of a plate with a paper towel underneath them to remove excess grease from the bottom. this will produce crispier chips.

6. In a small skillet on medium-high heat cook the ground sirloin, and season with the cumin, chile powder, onion powder, and garlic powder. cook thoroughly.

7. In a large bowl put the avocado spread on the bottom, then sour cream, then half of the shredded cheese.

8. Add in the ground sirloin, then cover in shredded cheeses, avocado, sour cream, and then top with the fire roasted tomatoes, sliced jalapeño, and sliced black olives.

TACO LIME SHRIMP

Servings: 4

Nutritional Facts Per Serving:			
Carbs:	5.3 g	Protein:	25 g
Fats:	8.3 g	Calories:	383 kcal

INGREDIENTS

1 lb medium shrimp, peeled and deveined

Juice of 2-3 limes, plus more wedges for serving

¼ cup enchilada sauce (see recipe in Mexican Essentials section)

2 tbsp taco seasoning (see recipe in Mexican Essentials section)

2 tbsp of your favorite oil

1 tsp garlic powder

Freshly ground black pepper

Freshly chopped cilantro, for garnish

This is how you make the recipe

1. In a large bowl, whisk together lime juice, enchilada sauce, taco seasoning, oil, and garlic powder and season with pepper. Add shrimp and toss until completely coated.

2. Marinate 20 minutes.

3. Heat grill to medium-high heat. Skewer shrimp and grill until pink and charred, 3 minutes per side.

4. Garnish with cilantro and squeeze with more lime before serving.

CHEDDAR WRAPPED TACO ROLLS

Servings: 4			
Nutritional Facts Per Serving:			
Carbs:	2 g	Protein:	37 g
Fats:	35 g	Calories:	491 kcal

INGREDIENTS

Crust:
2 cups grated cheddar cheese
Coconut oil

Filling:
1 cup ground beef
¼ cup tomatoes, chopped
½ avocado, chopped
2 tsp taco sauce (see recipe in Mexican Essentials section)

This is how you make the recipe

1. Preheat oven to 400°F.

2. Cover a small baking sheet with parchment paper leaving some on the sides to lift the cheese up and out when it's done.

3. Grease the parchment paper lightly with coconut oil.

4. Sprinkle shredded cheddar cheese to cover the baking sheet with one layer.

5. Bake 15 minutes, until it bubbles and browns on top.

6. Remove from oven and slide a silicone spatula under all the edges and under the middle. (If you cannot, continue baking them until you can.)

7. Add ground beef and cook for another 5-10 minutes.

8. Combine the rest of the toppings in a bowl.

9. Remove from oven and remove from baking pan by holding the sides of the parchment paper.

10. Add the cold toppings in a single layer.

11. Slice with pizza cutter into 4 slices. Roll each slice from bottom to top.

CHEESY TACO SKILLET

Servings: 6			
Nutritional Facts Per Serving:			
Carbs:	5 g	Protein:	32.7 g
Fats:	14.7 g	Calories:	292 kcal

INGREDIENTS

1 tbsp coconut oil

1 red bell pepper, chopped

¼ cup sliced green onions, plus more for garnish

2 cloves garlic, minced

1 tbsp chile powder

1 tbsp ground cumin

1 lb ground beef

1 (15-oz) can diced tomatoes

1 tbsp hot sauce

1 cup shredded Monterrey jack cheese

1 cup shredded cheddar

Sea salt

This is how you make the recipe

1. Heat up the oil in a large skillet over medium-high heat. Add bell pepper and green onions and cook until tender, 5 minutes. Add garlic and cook until fragrant, 1 minute. Add chile powder and cumin and stir until combined, then season with salt.

2. Add ground beef and cook until no longer pink, 5 minutes more.

3. Add diced tomatoes and stir until combined. Stir in hot sauce, Monterrey Jack, and cheddar. Cover with a lid and let melt, 2 minutes, then garnish with green onions and serve.

CHICKEN ENCHILADA BOWL

(Spanish: Enchilada = Seasoned with chile)

Servings: 4			
Nutritional Facts Per Serving:			
Carbs:	6.14 g	Protein:	38.38 g
Fats:	40.21 g	Calories:	568 kcal

INGREDIENTS

2 tbsp coconut oil

1 lb boneless, skinless chicken thighs

¾ cup red enchilada sauce (see recipe in Mexican Essentials section)

¼ cup water

¼ cup chopped onion

1- 4 oz can diced green chiles

Toppings:

1 whole avocado, diced

1 cup shredded Monterrey Jack cheese

¼ cup chopped pickled jalapeños

½ cup sour cream

1 Roma tomato, chopped

Optional: serve over arroz Mexicano for a more complete meal!

This is how you make the recipe

1. In a pot or dutch oven over medium heat melt the coconut oil. Once hot, sear chicken thighs until lightly brown.

2. Pour in enchilada sauce and water then add onion and green chiles. Reduce heat to a simmer and cover. Cook chicken for 17-25 minutes or until chicken is tender and fully cooked through to at least 165°F internal temperature.

3. Carefully remove the chicken and place onto a work surface. Chop or shred chicken (your preference) then add it back into the pot. Let the chicken simmer uncovered for an additional 10 minutes to absorb flavor and allow the sauce to reduce a little.

4. To Serve, top with avocado, cheese, jalapeño, sour cream, tomato, and any other desired toppings.

CHICKEN FAJITA BOWL
(Spanish: Fajita: little strips)

Servings: 4			
Nutritional Facts Per Serving:			
Carbs:	9 g	Protein:	41 g
Fats:	71 g	Calories:	862 kcal

INGREDIENTS

Tex-Mex seasoning:

3 tbsp chili powder

2 tbsp ground cumin

1 tbsp ground black pepper

1 tbsp salt

1 tbsp garlic powder

1½ tsp ground red pepper

Chicken Fajita Bowl:

10 oz romaine lettuce

5 oz cherry tomatoes

2 avocados

4 tbsp fresh cilantro

3 oz butter

1½ lbs boneless chicken thighs

2 tbsp Tex-Mex seasoning

1 yellow onion

1 green bell pepper

5 oz Mexican cheese

1 cup sour cream (optional)

salt and pepper

This is how you make the recipe

1. Prepare the toppings: Tear the lettuce, chop tomatoes, dice avocados, clean and chop the cilantro and grate the cheese. Set aside.

2. Slice onion and pepper fairly thin.

3. On a separate cutting board, cut the chicken into thin strips.

4. Fry the chicken in butter in a large skillet over medium-high heat. Salt and pepper to taste. When the chicken is almost cooked through, add onion, pepper and Tex-Mex seasoning.

5. Lower the heat and continue to fry while stirring for a couple of minutes until the chicken is thoroughly cooked and the veggies have softened just a bit.

6. Place lettuce in a bowl and add the chicken mixture. Add shredded cheese, diced avocado, chopped tomatoes, fresh cilantro and perhaps a dollop of sour cream.

AVOCADO POZOLE DE POLLO

(Spanish: pollo = chicken, Aztec: pozolli = hominy)

Servings: 6

Nutritional Facts Per Serving:

Carbs:	4 g	Protein:	18 g
Fats:	21 g	Calories:	410 kcal

INGREDIENTS

4 cups chicken stock

2 lbs boneless, skinless chicken thighs

2 Poblano peppers, sliced into large chunks

1 avocado, cubed or sliced

1 white onion, quartered

2 cloves garlic, minced

2 tbsp butter

1 tbsp cumin

1 tbsp oregano

1 tbsp pink Himalayan salt

2 tsp chile powder

fresh ground black pepper

fresh cilantro for garnish

This is how you make the recipe

1. Place all ingredients (except avocado) into a slow-cooker.

2. Cook on low for 6 - 8 hours or until chicken is cooked through and contains no pink.

3. Using a slotted spoon, remove and discard onion quarters and Poblano pepper chunks.

4. Remove chicken and shred in a separate bowl.

5. Place shredded chicken back into slow cooker and cook for an additional 30 minutes.

6. Ladle into serving bowls and garnish with avocado and enjoy!

CHICKEN QUESADILLA
(Spanish: Quesadilla = little cheesecake)

Servings: 2		
Nutritional Facts Per Serving:		
Carbs:	6.1 g	Protein: 52.7 g
Fats:	40.5 g	Calories: 599 kcal

INGREDIENTS

1½ cups mozzarella cheese, grated
1½ cups cheddar cheese, grated
1 cup cooked chicken
¼ cup bell pepper
¼ cup diced tomato
⅛ cup green onion
Sour cream
Salsa for serving (see recipe in Mexican Essentials section)
Guacamole for serving (see recipe in Mexican Essentials section)
Fresh basil, parsley or cilantro, chopped, as garnish

This is how you make the recipe

1. Preheat oven to 400°F. Cover a pizza pan with parchment paper. Mix the cheeses together, then evenly spread them over the parchment paper (in a circle shape). Bake the cheese shells for 5 minutes. Pour off any extra oil as soon as it comes out of the oven.

2. Place the chicken over half of the cheese shell. Then add the sliced peppers, diced tomato and the chopped green onion. Fold the cheese shell in half over the chicken and veggies. Press it firmly, then return it to the oven for another 4-5 minutes.

3. Serve with sour cream, salsa and guacamole. Garnish with chopped fresh basil, parsley or cilantro.

BEEF TAMALES
(Aztec: tamalli = wrapped)

Servings: 8

Nutritional Facts Per Serving:

Carbs:	4.5 g	Protein:	22.3 g
Fats:	20.5 g	Calories:	291 kcal

INGREDIENTS

1 package dried corn husks
Hot sauce, for serving (optional)
Salsa, for serving (optional) (see recipe in Mexican Essentials section)
Guacamole, for serving (optional) (see recipe in Mexican Essentials section)

Filling:
1 lb chuck roast
1 tbsp bacon fat
1 cup beef broth
1 clove garlic, minced
2 green chiles, roasted with skin and seeds removed, diced finely
½ tsp cumin
¼ tsp dried oregano
¼ tsp sea salt
¼ tsp ground black pepper
¼ tsp chile powder

Dough:
4 cups finely ground blanched almond flour
1 tsp sea salt
4 tbsp cold lard/bacon fat or tallow
¼ cup beef or chicken broth

This is how you make the recipe

Soak 8 corn husks in a bowl of very warm water.

1. Filling: Place a large skillet over medium-high heat. Add the bacon fat and allow to melt. Add the beef and brown on all sides.

2. Place beef and remaining ingredients in a slow cooker. Cook on low for about 4 hours or until the beef is tender and shreds easily.

3. When beef is done, remove from pot and save the liquid. Allow the beef to cool slightly before shredding with a fork.

4. Add the beef to a bowl and pour just enough of the saved liquid (about ½ cup) to make the beef moist but not soggy.

1. Dough: Add all of the dough ingredients to a medium sized mixing bowl and combine with a fork, making sure to break apart any clumps.

2. Set the dough aside for about 10 minutes.

1. To assemble the tamales: Place about ½ cup of dough in the center of a corn husk and spread around to form a square about ½ inch thick.

2. Place about 2 tbsp of filling in the center of the dough and gently fold the top and bottoms of the dough around the filling.

3. Fold the sides of the corn husk inward towards the center and then fold the top and bottom inward to form a rectangular shape.

4. Place a steaming basket into a large pot. Add enough water to the level just below the basket. Place the pot over medium-high heat.

5. Add the tamales to the steamer basket. Once the water starts to steam, cover the pot and turn the heat to low. Steam the tamales for 1 hour.

6. Take the tamales out of the pot and allow to sit for about 5 minutes. Unwrap the tamales and serve with salsa, guacamole, and/or your favorite hot sauce.

CHILI CON CARNE
(Aztec: chilli = pepper, Spanish: con carne = with meat))

Servings: 8			
Nutritional Facts Per Serving:			
Carbs:	3 g	Protein:	21 g
Fats:	19 g	Calories:	364 kcal

INGREDIENTS

3 tbsp coconut oil

1 small onion, diced

3 cloves garlic, crushed

2 small red chiles, finely chopped

1 tsp chile powder

1 tsp salt

2 lbs ground beef

2 tbsp tomato paste

1 tbsp paprika

1 tbsp cumin, ground

1 tbsp coriander, ground

1 lb canned diced tomatoes

½ tsp pepper

Sour cream

This is how you make the recipe

1. Heat the oil in a large saucepan over medium-high heat.

2. Add the onion, garlic, and chopped chiles and saute for 3-5 minutes until the onion is translucent.

3. Add the chile powder and salt and stir well.

4. Add the ground beef. Stir continuously to break apart the meat, saute for 10 minutes until the beef is well browned.

5. Add the tomato paste, paprika, cumin and coriander and stir well.

6. Cook for 5 minutes before adding the canned diced tomatoes and pepper. Mix well.

7. Reduce the heat to a low simmer and continue to cook, uncovered, for 20-30 minutes.

8. Taste your chile and add additional salt and pepper if desired. Serve immediately.

HORCHATA SMOOTHIE

Servings: 2			
Nutritional Facts Per Serving:			
Carbs:	5 g	Protein:	11.9 g
Fats:	22.2 g	Calories:	282 kcal

INGREDIENTS

2 handfuls of almonds, blanched

1 cup unsweetened almond milk

1 large egg

2 tbsp chia seeds

1 tbsp fresh lime zest

1 tsp cinnamon powder

1 whole cinnamon stick

4 tbsp Swerve

2 cups warm water

This is how you make the recipe

1. Place the blanched almonds, fresh lime zest and cinnamon stick in a bowl. Cover with 2 cups of warm water. Let stand for at least 8 hours or even better overnight.

2. After the nuts have soaked and softened, remove the cinnamon stick and lime zest.

3. Place the rest (almonds and water) into a small sauce pan. Add the almond milk and puree with a immersion blender until very smooth.

4. Heat the mixture up until it starts sizzling and add cinnamon and the Swerve.

5. Whisk the egg and pour it slowly into the mixture while stirring constantly to avoid clumping. Keep stirring and cook for a minute or two.

6. Take off the heat and mix in the chia seeds. Allow to thicken, pour in a glass and serve immediately or refrigerate and serve chilled. If you don't like the grainy texture of chia seeds, simply place in a blender and pulse until smooth.

MEXICAN CHOCOLATE MATCHA DRINK

Servings: 1			
Nutritional Facts Per Serving:			
Carbs:	3 g	Protein:	2 g
Fats:	3 g	Calories:	48 kcal

INGREDIENTS

⅛ tsp cinnamon

½ tsp matcha

1 tbsp coconut oil

1 tbsp cacao powder can substitute cocoa powder

8 oz boiling water

Pinch cayenne

Swerve to taste

Notes:

If you find it hard to measure the cayenne powder, just use a sprinkle instead.

This is how you make the recipe

1. Add all ingredients to a high-speed blender and blend on high.

2. Pour into you mug and enjoy!

MEXICAN HOT CHOCOLATE

Servings: 2

Nutritional Facts Per Serving:

Carbs:	3.8 g	Protein:	1.9 g
Fats:	18.2 g	Calories:	177 kcal

INGREDIENTS

1¼ cup almond milk

½ cup heavy cream

2 tbsp unsweetened cocoa powder

1 tbsp Swerve

¼ tsp ground cinnamon

⅛ to ¼ tsp chipotle powder

Dollop whipped cream and a sprinkle cinnamon for garnish

This is how you make the recipe

1. In a medium saucepan over medium heat, combine almond milk, cream, cocoa powder, Swerve, cinnamon and chipotle powder.

2. Whisk until well combined, then bring to a gentle simmer.

3. Remove from heat, divide between two mugs, and top with whipped cream and cinnamon.

4. For an extra kick, add a shot of strong coffee or espresso.

DINNER

[Typically, cena is a light meal or simply a soup or snack eaten late in the evening]

SOPA DE MARISCOS
(Spanish: Seafood soup)

Servings: 6

Nutritional Facts Per Serving:

Carbs:	9 g	Protein:	27 g
Fats:	14 g	Calories:	284 kcal

INGREDIENTS

Soup:

10 oz wild caught cod

8 oz calamari

8 oz shrimp, peeled and deveined

¼ cup coconut oil

1½ cup tomato sauce

½ cup coconut cream

1 qt seafood broth

2 cups water

3 medium carrots

4 stalks celery

4 stalks green onion

4 cloves garlic

1 medium onion

8 oz mushrooms

1 lime

1 lemon

Spices:

1 tbsp salt

2 tsp pepper

2 tsp red pepper flakes

1 tsp thyme

1 tsp dill

3 whole bay leaves

2 tsp basil

2 tsp oregano

fresh parsley

This is how you make the recipe

1. Put the coconut oil in a soup pot on medium heat.

2. Throw in onions and crushed garlic to cook until fragrant.

3. Then throw in chopped carrots and celery. Let these veggies cook down until tender.

4. Pour in 1 qt of broth, water and tomato sauce.

5. Let this come to a boil, then reduce heat to a simmer. Allow the veggies and broth to simmer for about 30 minutes.

6. Add the spices.

7. While the soup is simmering, cut your calamari tubes into about ½ inch long pieces and let them sit in a bowl with lemon juice. The lemon juice will help prevent them turning rubbery if cooked too long.

8. Chop up mushrooms and add them to the soup after it's been simmering for 30 minutes. Add the coconut cream. Make sure the soup returns to a simmer if cooled off too much by the cream.

9. When the mushrooms have been cooking for about 10 minutes, add in the cod and let it cook for about 10 minutes.

10. Take a wooden spoon and break the fish into smaller pieces.

11. To cook the shrimp, make sure the water is simmering and turn up the heat just a little bit. Add them in at the same time and let them cook for about 3 minutes.

12. Add in the calamari (don't add the lemon juice) to the soup and let the entire soup cook for another 2 minutes. If you let it cook for longer , the calamari may become rubbery and the shrimp hard.

13. Turn off the stove and take the pot off the heat. Remove the bay leaf. Add in the lime juice, to taste.

TACO SOUP

Servings: 3			
Nutritional Facts Per Serving:			
Carbs:	11 g	Protein:	8 g
Fats:	14 g	Calories:	201 kcal

INGREDIENTS

2 tbsp butter

1 medium green pepper, diced

1 clove garlic, crushed

1 tsp oregano, dried

1 tsp cumin, ground

1 tsp paprika, ground

8 oz tomato puree

2 cups chicken stock

5 oz pork, shredded or pulled

1 tsp pepper

½ tsp salt

½ cup cheddar cheese, grated

½ medium avocado, diced

3 tsp cilantro, finely shredded

3 tbsp sour cream

This is how you make the recipe

1. In a large saucepan place the butter, diced pepper and garlic and saute over medium heat for 3 minutes, until the butter is bubbling.

2. Add the oregano, cumin and paprika and saute for a further 3 minutes, until fragrant.

3. Add the tomato puree and chicken stock and bring to a simmer.

4. Add the pork, salt and pepper. Simmering for 2 minutes to ensure the pork is heated through.

5. Ladle the soup into three bowls and garnish with the shredded cheddar, diced avocado, cilantro, and sour cream.

ALBONDIGAS SOUP
(Spanish: albondigas = meatballs)

Servings: 6		
Nutritional Facts Per Serving:		
Carbs:	7 g	Protein:	22 g
Fats:	22 g	Calories:	319 kcal

INGREDIENTS

2 tbsp avocado oil

1 yellow onion, diced

4 garlic cloves, minced

2 whole bay leaves

1 (28-oz) can diced tomatoes

1 cup chipolata salsa

32 oz beef broth

1 lb ground beef

½ lb chorizo

1 egg

¼ cup half & half

6 tbsp almond flour

½ tsp cumin

½ tsp salt

⅓ cup chopped cilantro, plus more for serving

This is how you make the recipe

1. Heat oil in a large heavy pot over medium heat. Add the diced onion and saute until soft. Add the garlic and cook for 1 minute more. Add the diced tomatoes, salsa, beef broth, and bay leaves. Reduce heat and let simmer.

2. Combine the beef, chorizo, almond flour, egg, half & half, cumin, salt, and chopped cilantro in a large bowl and mix until just combined. Shape into 2 balls and set aside.

3. Add meatballs to soup, cover and let simmer for 20 minutes. Remove the bay leaves and ladle soup into bowls. Avoid stirring the soup after adding the meatballs so they do not break apart.

4. Serve with extra cilantro.

DESSERTS

MEXICAN CREAMY FLAN

Servings: 4			
Nutritional Facts Per Serving:			
Carbs:	15.4 g	Protein:	4.1 g
Fats:	17.3 g	Calories:	177 kcal

INGREDIENTS

4 tbsp Swerve
¼ cup water
1 tbsp butter
1 cup heavy cream
1 tsp vanilla
2 whole eggs
1 egg yolk

This is how you make the recipe

1. In a deep pan, heat up the 4 tbsp Swerve and water on medium-low heat. Bring it to a simmer before adding in your butter.

2. Stir occasionally until it becomes a dark amber color… but make sure it doesn't burn as it can burn easily!

3. Once you have a nice amber color, scoop your caramel into three ramekins. Let it sit and cool.

4. In a bowl, mix your cream, 4 tbsp Swerve and vanilla. Stir until the Swerve has dissolved.

5. In another bowl, whisk together your eggs and egg yolk. Slowly whisk this mix into your cream mix, stirring until the egg and cream are 1 liquid (the egg whites don't clump together)

6. Pour your cream into the ramekins on top of the caramel. Place your ramekins into a casserole dish and fill it with boiling water

7. Bake at 350°F for about 45-50 minutes, until the flan is set. It should have a wobbly center and a firm surface. Overcooking leads to bubbles.

8. Take them out and let cool.

9. When ready to serve, take a knife and gently slice them free of the ramekins.

10. Turn them upside down on a plate and jiggle it lightly until it plops right out on the plate! The caramel should ooze out as well.

MEXICAN PUDDING

Servings: 2			
Nutritional Facts Per Serving:			
Carbs:	5.7 g	Protein:	4.2 g
Fats:	16.2 g	Calories:	195 kcal

INGREDIENTS

1 large overripe avocado

¼ cup Dutch process cocoa powder

¼ cup Swerve confectioners

1½ tsp cinnamon

⅛ - ¼ tsp cayenne pepper

¼ tsp sugar-free vanilla extract

This is how you make the recipe

1. Place all ingredients into a blender and process until smooth.

2. Spoon into 2 (4-oz) jars and serve immediately or refrigerate.

3. To store, refrigerate sealed of covered with cling film for up to two days.

MEXICAN VANILLA ICE CREAM WITH STRAWBERRIES

Servings: 2			
Nutritional Facts Per Serving:			
Carbs:	1.8 g	Protein:	0.1 g
Fats:	25 g	Calories:	252 kcal

INGREDIENTS

2 eggs
1¼ cups heavy whipping cream
1 each vanilla bean substitute with
½ tsp vanilla extract
2 tbsp Swerve confectioners
1 tsp ground cinnamon
1 pinch ground nutmeg
1 pinch cayenne pepper
2 oz strawberries, sliced

This is how you make the recipe

1. Separate the eggs. Whisk the egg yolks until smooth and fluffy. Set the egg whites aside.

2. In a saucepan, combine the cream with the vanilla and the Swerve. Bring to a boil and simmer for a few minutes, until the cream thickens slightly.

3. Add 1 tbsp ground cinnamon, 1 pinch of ground nutmeg, and 1 pinch of cayenne pepper to the mixture and stir

4. Reduce the heat and pour the whipped egg yolks into the hot cream. Combine well and let it simmer on low heat while stirring constantly, until the mixture thickens.

5. Refrigerate mixture until cool.

6. Beat the egg whites until stiff and fluffy; fold into the cream mixture.

7. Pour the batter into a ice cream maker or in a jar with a lid and place in the freezer. Stir occasionally and continue freezing until it reaches desired consistency.

8. When ice cream is ready to serve, top with slices of strawberry.

MEXICAN WEDDING COOKIES

Servings: 24			
Nutritional Facts Per Serving:			
Carbs:	1 g	Protein:	1 g
Fats:	7 g	Calories:	73 kcal

INGREDIENTS

7 tbsp pecans
4¼ oz almond flour
¼ tsp kosher salt
4 oz butter, room temperature
¼ cup Swerve confectioners
1 tsp sugar-free vanilla extract

Powdered 'sugar' coating:
Swerve confectioners
pinch ground cinnamon

This is how you make the recipe

1. Add pecans to a food processor and process until finely ground. Be careful you don't over-blend or you'll end up with pecan butter!

2. Add pecan flour and almond flour to a skillet or pan, and toast over medium heat until golden and fragrant (3-6 minutes). Remove from pan, whisk in salt and set aside to cool completely (very important!).

3. Cream butter in a large bowl with an electric mixer, 2-3 minutes. Add in Swerve and continue to beat until thoroughly mixed and much of the Swerve has dissolved. Add in vanilla extract and beat until just combined.

4. With your mixer on low, add in half of your nut flour mixture- mixing until just incorporated. Mix in the rest.

5. Wrap cookie dough with cling film (saran wrap) and refrigerate for at least an hour.

6. Preheat oven to 350°F and line a baking tray with parchment paper.

7. Divide dough into 24 small round cookies. Place rounds on the prepared baking tray and place in the freezer for 15 minutes prior to baking.

8. Bake for 13-15 minutes. The cookies will be deep golden, but very soft and fragile to touch. Sieve a touch of powdered Swerve with cinnamon on top immediately (it'll dissolve into the warm cookies).

9. Allow to cool for 15 more minutes before adding more powdered Swerve and cinnamon. The cookies will become less fragile as they cool. Store in an airtight container for up to 1 week.

TRES LECHES CAKE
(Spanish: tres leches = three milks)

Servings: 16			
Nutritional Facts Per Serving:			
Carbs:	3 g	Protein:	7 g
Fats:	24 g	Calories:	275 kcal

INGREDIENTS

Cake:
8 eggs
1⅓ cups Swerve
2 tsp vanilla
½ cup unsweetened almond milk
½ cup almond flour
½ cup coconut flour
½ cup ground golden flax or
additional almond flour
1½ tsp baking powder
¼ tsp salt
Coconut oil

Topping:
1 recipe sugar-free sweetened
condensed milk (see below)
⅓ cup half & half

Icing:
1 pint heavy cream
⅓ cup Swerve

Sugar-Free Condensed Milk:
¼ cup heavy cream
2 tbsp butter
½ cup Swerve
1 egg yolk

This is how you make the recipe

1. First, make the sugar-free condensed milk by placing the heavy cream, Swerve and butter to a gentle boil and cook stirring frequently until it is light golden brown and thick enough to coat the back of a spoon. Remove from heat and let cool to room temperature before stirring in the egg yolk.

2. Pour the sweetened condensed milk into a heatproof container and cool in the fridge. The mixture will thicken up as it cools. You can use the mixture after 1 hour.

3. Preheat oven to 350°F. Grease a 9 x 13 inch pan with coconut oil.

4. Beat eggs with ½ cup Swerve. Stir in almond milk and vanilla. Add baking mix, baking powder, and salt and mix until just combined. Pour into prepared pan and spread to even out the surface.

5. Bake for 40 to 45 minutes or until golden and slightly firm to the touch in the middle. Cool to room temperature.

6. Combine condensed milk and half & half in a small measuring cup. When cake is cool, gently pierce the surface with a fork every inch or so. Slowly drizzle on the sweetened condensed milk and half & half mixture.

7. Allow the cake to absorb the milk mixture for 30 minutes. Meanwhile whip the cream. When stiff peaks form add the Swerve. Spread over the surface of the cake, after it has absorbed the condensed milk. Store in the fridge.

CHOCOLATE AVOCADO CAKE

Servings: 12		
Nutritional Facts Per Serving:		
Carbs:	6.9 g	Protein:	7.6 g
Fats:	15.6 g	Calories:	207 kcal

INGREDIENTS

Cake:
2 cups almond flour
½ cup unsweetened cocoa powder
½ cup Swerve
1 tsp baking soda
1 avocado
½ cup dairy-free coconut yogurt
½ cup almond milk
2 eggs
1 tsp vanilla extract
Coconut oil

Chocolate Avocado Frosting:
½ avocado
2 tbsp coconut cream
2 tbsp unsweetened cocoa powder
2 tbsp Swerve
2 tbsp coconut oil, melted
⅛ tsp salt

This is how you make the recipe

1. Place all of the chocolate avocado frosting ingredients in a blender or food processor.

2. Blend until it forms a chocolate frosting with no lumps of avocado. You may have to stop your blender every 20 seconds, scrap down the bowl with a spatula and repeat until your thick shiny chocolate frosting forms with no lumps.

3. Preheat oven to 350˚F. Grease a 8 inch round cake pan with coconut oil, set aside.

4. In a large mixing bowl, combine all the cake dry ingredients: almond flour, unsweetened cocoa powder, Swerve and baking soda. Set aside.

5. In a blender or food processor, add all the cake wet ingredients: avocado, yogurt, almond milk, eggs and vanilla.

6. Blend until a smooth batter forms with no lumps of avocado (about 45 seconds on high-speed.)

7. Pour the liquid mixture onto the dry mixture and combine with a spatula until it forms a consistent chocolate cake batter.

8. Transfer the cake batter into the prepared round cake pan.

9. Bake for 30-40 minutes or until a skewer inserted in the middle of the cake comes out clean. Check the cooking every 5 minutes after the first 25 minutes cooking time to make sure your cake comes out perfectly.

10. Cool down on a wire rack for about an hour before spreading the chocolate avocado frosting on top.

11. Spread the chocolate frosting on top of your cooled chocolate avocado cake.

12. Place the completed cake in the freezer for 10 minutes to set the frosting better and produce a really fudgy cake texture. Serve and enjoy!

Go to **www.ketoveo.com** for more guides and resources to help you on your keto journey.

Made in the USA
San Bernardino, CA
04 December 2019